The **Good** Book

PARTICIPANT'S GUIDE

The **Good** Book

PARTICIPANT'S GUIDE

40 Chapters That Reveal the Bible's Biggest Ideas

DERON SPOO

WITH KEVIN AND SHERRY HARNEY

David C Cook®

transforming lives together

THE GOOD BOOK PARTICIPANT'S GUIDE
Published by David C Cook
4050 Lee Vance Drive
Colorado Springs, CO 80918 U.S.A.

David C Cook U.K., Kingsway Communications
Eastbourne, East Sussex BN23 6NT, England

The graphic circle C logo is a registered trademark of David C Cook.

All Scripture quotations are taken from the Christian Standard Bible®, Copyright
© 2017 by Holman Bible Publishers. Used by permission. Christian Standard
Bible® and CSB® are federally registered trademarks of Holman Bible Publishers.

ISBN 978-1-4347-1025-3
eISBN 978-1-4347-1105-2

© 2017 Deron Spoo
Published in association with the literary agency of Ann Spangler &
Company, 1415 Laurel Avenue Southeast, Grand Rapids, Michigan 49506.

The Team: Tim Peterson, Kevin Harney, Nick Lee, Jennifer Lonas,
Helen Macdonald, Abby DeBenedittis, Susan Murdock
Cover Design: Amy Konyndyk
Cover Photo: Getty Images

Printed in the United States of America
First Edition 2017

1 2 3 4 5 6 7 8 9 10

011217

Contents

Preface

More than two decades ago, George Hunter coined a term for people with no God history and "no christian memory." Based on the word *agnostic*, a term for those who view God as unknowable, Hunter came up with the word *ignostic* to describe someone who is ignorant about the subject of God.[1] An ignostic may willingly admit that God is knowable, but he or she doesn't have the first clue about how or where to begin a search for him.

If the Bible intimidates even the most adept readers, imagine how intimidating it would seem to a first-time Bible reader. On top of that, the Bible is notoriously easy to misinterpret, especially when lone verses are lifted out of context.

Scripture is an infinite resource for knowing God and understanding life, but practically speaking, where should a new Bible reader begin? And how can anyone decipher the bizarre names, faraway places, and foreign cultures of the distant past? Who is qualified to guide us in our quest to grasp the simple truths of God's love, the necessity of a life-changing experience with him, and the promise of forgiveness and a fresh start?

---

1   George G. Hunter III, *How to Reach Secular People* (Nashville: Abingdon Press, 1992), 41.

The Bible is like the ocean, according to an old metaphor. The ocean is so deep in places that no person, however capable a swimmer, could survive its extremities. But at the same time, when the ocean touches the land, the water is so shallow and the waves lapping the beach are so gentle that even a toddler can safely play there. Anyone who has visited the beach has seen firsthand that the ocean is both intimidating and approachable.

The same is true of the Bible. Like the ocean, its depths can never be fathomed. Even after a lifetime of study, the most brilliant theologians admit they've only begun to plumb its depths. Centuries of Christian scholarship haven't been able to chart its vast expanse. The Bible can be intimidating and yet approachable at the same time. Anyone can pick up a Bible and encounter simple truths that are nothing short of life changing.

This eight-week study is a companion to *The Good Book* video series and book. These resources are designed to help two distinct groups of people. In the first group are those who have faith in Jesus and have spent a good deal of time reading the Bible. For you I offer a word of advice: Reject the tendency to be satisfied with your current understanding of the Bible. Refuse the temptation to think that what you grasp of the Scriptures today is somehow enough. Don't just settle for wading in the surf. Dive deeper! Untold riches await your discovery.

In the second group are those who are just beginning their study of the Bible. My advice for you? Start right where you are. Dip your toe in the water. Wade up to your knees. Take your time.

I believe you'll find yourself longing to dive deeper as you walk through these eight sessions.

The goal of these studies is to give the big picture and the general structure of the Bible, God's Good Book. Although they aren't exhaustive, they go deep. My prayer is that you'll discover the beauty, life, and power of God in the pages of the Bible. As you do, may you encounter the God who made you, loves you, and offers salvation in the name of his only Son, Jesus Christ.

With you on the journey,

Deron Spoo

SESSION 1

In the Beginning

The central character at the start of the Bible is God. No question about it. He is the one who spoke all things into existence. God is the focal point of the whole biblical story from Genesis to Revelation. Our story makes sense only when we realize that he is the creator and that we are his beloved children, created in his image.

THE BIG PICTURE

Session Title: In the Beginning

The Story Line: Out of nothing God spoke and created everything. He made the heavens and the earth. He shaped man and woman and breathed life into them. When everything broke because of sin and rebellion, God began a plan to restore his children to relationship with him and one another. Then he formed a nation of people to call his own and bless. His desire was that they would follow him with such authentic faith that they would become a blessing to all the nations of the world.

The Time Line: Creation to around 2000 BC

Key Book:
- Genesis

Key Themes:
- Everything God created is good.
- Our rebellion against God was costly.
- The wonder of God's plan to restore humanity fills us with awe.
- God calls his people to step out in faith.
- Becoming more like Christ isn't easy, but it's our destiny.

Key Characters:
- God, the creator and sustainer of all things
- Adam and Eve
- The Devil
- Noah and his family
- Abraham and Sarah
- Isaac

Prayer Direction:
- Thank God for the beauty and glory of his creation, including you and the people around you.
- Confess the greatness of your sin, and thank God that his grace is always enough.

• Ask for boldness to live with confident faith, no matter what you face.

INTRODUCTION

Ready, Set, Go!

A group of grade-school students crouch at the starting line for a race during their physical-education class. The teacher says slowly and deliberately, "Ready … set … GO!" In one moment all the kids lunge forward in an effort to get a good start in the race. They know that the first few seconds of a sprint can make all the difference in the world.

A young couple stands at the altar and promises, "For better, for worse, for richer, for poorer, in sickness and in health, as long as we both shall live." The next few months will set the tone for the coming years of their relationship. Graciousness, patience, and tenderness set a trajectory for relational health and marital success. Selfishness, irritability, and impatience can launch a couple into marital conflict and dark days. The beginning is more important than most of us recognize at the time.

A speaker stands at a podium, opens his mouth, and begins his address. The introductory words and the first minute often tell the whole story. The listeners are gripped and engaged. Or their minds begin to wander. The start isn't just significant; it's a matter of communicational life and death.

"In the beginning God created the heavens and the earth" (Gen. 1:1). What a start! The opening words of the Bible paint a picture of a powerful, engaged, and creative God shaping the heavens, the stars, the earth, the animals, and finally, us. If we want to understand the story of the Bible and see the heart of God, it all begins here.

TALK ABOUT IT

Tell about a time you started well. How did your good start lead to a positive experience?

Or

Tell about a time you started poorly and describe how this poor start cost you in the end.

> *Christlikeness is not accomplished casually. It is*
> *rarely convenient, and it requires risk.*

VIDEO TEACHING NOTES

The Bible can be an intimidating book

Stephanie's story

The goodness of God's creation

The wrecking ball of sin

Erik's story

God calls his people to step out in bold faith

The call to sacrifice

The sacrifice of Jesus and the call to Christlikeness

VIDEO DISCUSSION

1. Tell about a struggle you had (or have) with the Bible and how you're seeking to resolve it. What do you hope will happen in your heart and life through your study of *The Good Book*?

2. Tell about your experience and journey with the Bible growing up and through this point in your life. What has helped your growth in understanding God's Word? What has hindered it?

Remember that the ultimate benefit of reading the Scriptures isn't greater familiarity with the Bible but deeper intimacy with God.

3. Tell about a time you felt abandoned or forsaken as you walked through life. How did God show his grace and presence during this difficult time?

Read Genesis 3:1–19.

4. Sin always has costs and consequences. What were some of the consequences Adam and Eve faced because of their sin?

5. What were some of the tactics you see Satan using to entice Adam and Eve into sinful choices? How does the Enemy still use these tactics today?

Testing is God's method of bringing out our best, while tempting is Satan's method of reducing us to our worst.

6. We're created in the image of God. What aspects of his image do you think he wants to see reflected in your life?

> *Faith isn't about perfection; it's about making*
> *continual progress in our relationship with God.*

Read Genesis 6:5–10, 22.

7. We live in a fallen and sin-stained world. What are some of the daily reminders that sin is still affecting creation, culture, and our lives?

8. Noah had faith and built the ark, just as the Lord commanded. In the video we learned about Erik, who was confident that God was leading him to help start a Christian school in his community. Tell about a time you followed the Lord's leading, taking a bold step of faith and doing something for him (small or large). What happened as a result of your obedience to God's leading?

> *God regularly calls his people to step out in faith*
> *for ends we cannot accomplish on our own.*

Read Genesis 12:1–9.

9. Like Abram and Sarai, imagine leaving everyone and everything you've ever known. What do you think might have been going through their minds and hearts? Leaving a home or place that's familiar, loved, and full of memories is hard for anyone. Tell about a time you had to make a hard move and leave a place (and people) behind. How did this experience affect your heart and faith?

10. Some people view faith as agreement with specific doctrines or intellectual beliefs and nothing more. Others see it as core beliefs that shape their lives and transform their daily actions. What is the difference between these two understandings of faith?

Read Genesis 22:1–14.

11. Abraham is a powerful example of how God calls his people to wait patiently for him to reveal his plan and will for their lives. Tell about an area of your life where you're waiting for God to lead you. How is he growing your faith during this season of waiting?

12. What is God calling you to do today to become more like Jesus? How can group members support and pray for you?

When God invites us into the adventure of following him, he rarely tells us where we'll end up. The only way to discover the end of the story is to take the first step.

CLOSING PRAYER

Take time as a group to pray in some of the following directions …

- Thank God for the beauty, majesty, and wonder of his creation. Be sure to thank him for the people he has placed in your life.
- Lift up prayers of thanksgiving for the people God has used to teach you his Word, the Bible.

- Confess the reality of sin and brokenness in our world and in your own life.
- Ask God to help you live with a deep conviction that he can use you, and other people, who are imperfect and in the process of growing in Christlikeness.
- Pray for the power of the Holy Spirit to help you grow to be more like Jesus with each passing day.
- Commit to sacrifice anything God calls you to surrender as you follow Jesus and grow in faith.

God is in no way limited by what we believe is possible.

Between Sessions

PERSONAL REFLECTION

Take time for personal reflection, and think about the following questions ...

How did God show his redemptive grace and unveil his plan of salvation in the opening book of the Bible?

What are areas God is growing you in Christlikeness (becoming more like Jesus)? How are you resisting the leading of God's Spirit, and how can you surrender more humbly to him?

When did you take a big risk because you felt God was calling you to be bold in faith? How did God show up and move in this situation? How did this experience grow your faith?

We never coast into Christlikeness.

PERSONAL PRAYER JOURNEY

In the space below, write a prayer for the members of your group, asking God to help each person become more like Jesus, even through the hard times in life.

_____

_____

_____

_____

Write a prayer thanking God for creating you in his image. Ask him to make you more like Jesus and grow you in areas of your faith where you feel you need to mature.

_____

_____

_____

_____

The fact that we have a designer
leads us to the truth that we
were also given a destiny.

PERSONAL ACTIONS

The Journey to Christlikeness

In the video, Deron says, "Christlikeness doesn't happen casually; [it] is not convenient.... We do not coast into Christlikeness." It's a lifelong journey that takes humility, courage, and a willingness to follow Jesus moment by moment.

Think back on your life and reflect on two areas where you felt convicted and called to grow in Christlikeness. Then write down your thoughts in the space provided.

I felt called to grow to be more like Jesus in this area:

_____

Reflect on specific steps you took as you sought to follow God's will and ways in this area of spiritual growth.

- _____
- _____
- _____
- _____

What challenges did you have to overcome to grow in Christlikeness in this area? What hurdles or obstacles did you face?

- _____
- _____
- _____
- _____

Every time we're faithful to take steps of obedience and push through the obstacles we face, God shows up and does great things in us, through us, and around us. Write down some of the amazing things God has been doing in response to your commitment to grow in Christlikeness in this area of your life.

- _____
- _____
- _____
- _____

Write a prayer of praise to God for helping you grow to be more like Jesus in this area of your life. Ask him to help you continue growing and pressing forward as well.

_____

_____

_____

_____

I also felt called to grow to be more like Jesus in this area:

_____

Reflect on specific steps you took as you sought to follow God's will and ways in this area of spiritual growth.

- _____
- _____
- _____
- _____

What challenges did you have to overcome to grow in Christlikeness in this area? What hurdles or obstacles did you face?

- _____
- _____
- _____
- _____

Every time we're faithful to take steps of obedience and push through the obstacles we face, God shows up and does great things in us, through us, and around us. Write down some of the amazing things God has been doing in response to your commitment to grow in Christlikeness in this area of your life.

- _____
- _____
- _____
- _____

Write a prayer of praise to God for helping you grow to be more like Jesus in this area of your life. Ask him to help you continue growing and pressing forward as well.

_____

_____

_____

_____

_____

True Beliefs and Actions

Authentic faith doesn't just believe something; it lets what we believe transform our lives, change our attitudes, and shape our futures. Adam and Eve learned this the hard way. Noah put faith into action, and it saved his life and family. Abraham put his faith into action and met God in a personal and powerful way. If we want to encounter God, we'll learn to hold on to what we believe with deep conviction and let our faith transform our actions and life choices.

Reflect on some of the things we're taught to believe in these opening chapters of the Bible, and write down some of the actions that should naturally flow from these faith-filled beliefs.

If I believe God is the creator of all things and his creation (including people) matters to him, these are some of the **actions** that should mark my life:

- _____
- _____
- _____
- _____

If I believe God can redeem, heal, and use the most broken people for his glory, these are some of the **actions** that should mark my life:

- _____
- _____
- _____
- _____

If I believe God speaks to people, leads them, and empowers them to accomplish things that exceed their own abilities, these are some of the **actions** that should mark my life:

- _____
- _____
- _____
- _____

If I believe Christlikeness takes time, work, and personal engagement, these are some of the **actions** that should mark my life:

- _____
- _____
- _____
- _____

Waiting Is More Than Waiting … a Lot More!

Abraham spent a lot of time waiting for God to do something. God's promises weren't answered in weeks, months, or years. Abraham waited for decades! During this season of waiting, God was working in Abraham's life.

What is something you've been waiting for? How long have you been waiting? What has God been doing in you during this season of waiting?

How can you pray with greater confidence and trust as you follow Jesus, even when his answers are veiled? How can you surrender

more fully to Jesus as you patiently await God's answer to your
prayers?

> *True faith is when we're willing to obey God even*
> *when we don't understand his ways.*

DEEPER LEARNING

As you reflect on what God has been teaching you during this
session, review the introduction and chapters 1–5 of *The Good
Book*.

JOURNAL, REFLECTIONS, AND NOTES

_____

_____

_____

_____

_____

_____

_____

_____

_____

_____

_____

_____

_____

_____

_____

_____

_____

_____

_____

_____

_____

_____

_____

SESSION 2

God Is Good When Life Gets Messy

Life can get messy, and we can find ourselves in trouble, conflict, and bondage of all sorts. The good news is, our God is in the business of delivering his people from any and every kind of mess. All through the Bible, God shows his power and desire to set his people free. No matter what ensnares, imprisons, or entangles you, God is ready to deliver!

THE BIG PICTURE

Session Title: God Is Good When Life Gets Messy

The Story Line: God's people were in bondage. They weren't facing small irritations or the ordinary struggles of life. They were prisoners in a foreign land. They were being beaten and abused and had no hope of deliverance from any human perspective. God's people were slaves laboring under harsh taskmasters in Egypt. Out of this seemingly hopeless situation, God showed up, spoke up, moved in power, and set his people free. Through heavenly power and in astounding ways, God made a way where there seemed to be none.

The Time Line: 1800 BC to 1050 BC

Key Books:
- Exodus
- Judges
- 1 Samuel

Key Themes:
- People often end up in bondage to something.
- God is ready and able to set us free. He is in the deliverance business.
- God is our provider.
- God remains faithful in our faithlessness.
- God delights when we seek to be faithful to him.

Key Characters:
- Moses
- Pharaoh
- Samson
- David

Prayer Direction:
- Confess to God the areas of bondage in your life and the ways you feel enslaved.

- Cry out to God for his presence and power to set you free.
- Thank God for his amazing faithfulness throughout history and in your own life.
- Pray for power to remain faithful to the God who is faithful to you.

INTRODUCTION

Facing the Mess

The history of the Bible is profoundly messy! If you or I had written the Bible, we would have been tempted to clean things up a bit and present a prettier picture. But God tells the human story as it really was and is—messy. Just think about it: from start to finish, God's best people had to wade through the confusion, chaos, and rubble of human brokenness and sin.

> *Adam* and *Eve* rebelled against God, blamed others, and got kicked out of Paradise.
>
> *Cain*, one of their sons, killed his brother.
>
> *Abraham* lied and pretended his wife was his sister.
>
> *Sarah* drove her handmaiden, Hagar (and Hagar's son), into the wilderness to die.
>
> *Jacob* deceived his father, Isaac, and stole his brother's blessing.
>
> *Moses* committed murder and tried to cover his tracks.

Samson battled with lust and temper and showed poor judgment.

Eli the prophet had an out-of-control family.

Saul the king lost his throne because he arrogantly assumed the role of prophet.

David took another man's wife and had her husband killed.

Solomon's wisdom was compromised because he married nonbelieving women.

Every *king of the northern kingdom* (Israel) did evil in the eyes of the Lord.

Many *kings of the southern kingdom* (Judah) embraced idol worship.

Jonah ran from God.

Judas Iscariot, one of the twelve disciples, betrayed the Savior.

Peter denied Jesus in his moment of greatest need.

Thomas doubted.

All the disciples ran away when the heat was on.

Paul persecuted Christians before he came to faith in Jesus.

If you're looking for tidy lives and clean portfolios, don't read the Bible. God tells it like it is. Most of the people who followed him in biblical times learned what we all discover with time: our lives will be messy, but God is good … all the time!

TALK ABOUT IT

Why do you think the Bible is so honest about the frailties, struggles, rebellion, and sins of God's people?

Or

What is one biblical story where God used a messy person and situation to accomplish his purposes? How does this biblical account inspire you as you follow Jesus and live for him in our messy world?

God remains faithful even in our unfaithfulness.

VIDEO TEACHING NOTES

John's story

The story of Moses and the exodus

Jamie's story

God's commands may keep us from experiencing short-term pleasure, but they lead us to long-term joy

The Ten Commandments:

- A right relationship with God (commandments one through four)
- A right relationship with other people (commandments five through ten)
- Foreshadowing the Great Commandments

The time of the judges (Samson)

The time of the kings (David)

VIDEO DISCUSSION

1. Tell about a time you faced unexpected loss, pain, or deep struggle in your life. How did God show up and help you through that messy time?

Our obedience to God is the secret to a life well lived.

2. In the video, John talked about waiting on God and trusting him even when the future looked bleak and there seemed to be little hope of finding a good job. What can help us wait with faithful hope, even when we can't see God's answer or solution on the horizon?

Every day we get to choose if we'll live a life of obedience
to God's Word and alignment with his will.

3. God is our rescuer, redeemer, provider, and deliverer. How have you experienced this in your life? How have you seen this proved true in the lives of other people? What situation are you presently encountering in which you need to experience God as rescuer, redeemer, provider, or deliverer? How can group members pray for you during this time?

Read Exodus 3:1–15.

4. How are God's presence, power, and provision revealed in this passage?

God's commands may keep us from short-term
pleasure, but they lead us to long-term joy.

5. If God hadn't appeared to Moses in the burning bush, where might the Israelites have ended up? If God hadn't shown up in your life and delivered you through Jesus, where might you be today?

6. In Exodus 14:14, Moses told the people to "be quiet" in the middle of a very hard time. What helps you be quiet and wait on God during the hard times in your life? Why is this so counterintuitive? In what specific and practical ways can we grow in trust and quietness as we live for Jesus?

Being quiet in the middle of a mess requires great courage and faith.

Read Exodus 20:1–17.
7. In Jamie's story, we meet a man who took countercultural actions to obey the commands of God instead of following the ways of the world. He moved out of his girlfriend's place to live in purity. How did his culturally strange decision have a gospel impact on other people? Tell about a time you decided to live for God in a way others thought was strange. How did God use this decision to shine his light and show people the presence and power of Jesus?

8. What short-term pleasures and payoffs have you forsaken and missed out on as a result of deciding to follow God's ways, the

truth of his Word, and his plan for your life? How have these same decisions led to long-term joy, blessings, and health?

God's presence is our greatest source of confidence and courage.

9. What do the Ten Commandments reveal about the character and heart of God? How are these commandments an expression of grace?

10. How might our faith and intimacy with God flourish if we passionately followed the first four of the Ten Commandments? Which of these commandments do you need to pay more attention to? What steps can you take to obey it more passionately? How would our relationships with others grow and become healthier if we took the final six of the Ten Commandments more seriously and sought to develop them in our lives? Which of these commandments do you need to tune in to and seek to live out with greater intentionality?

All of life is about relationships.

Read Judges 2:10–17.

11. How is our world a lot like the time of the judges? What cycle did the Israelites repeat over and over? Why is this cycle so dangerous, and how can it show up in our lives?

12. Samson's life motto could have been "How far can I go?" His goal was always to push the boundaries and test God's patience

when it came to his personal disobedience. David, though he was human and made mistakes, lived a very different way. His life motto could have been "How faithful can I be?" He spent most of his life striving to walk in the ways of the Lord, and when he messed up, he was quick to sincerely repent. What are some of the qualities that mark the life of a person with a "How far can I go?" attitude? What characteristics do you see in the life of a person who has a "How faithful can I be?" attitude? Identify one area of your life in which you're striving to be more faithful to Jesus.

The Ten Commandments challenge us to live beyond what feels good to what God has revealed as good.

CLOSING PRAYER

Take time as a group to pray in some of the following directions …

- Thank God for the ways he has been your deliverer, provider, redeemer, and rescuer.
- Lift up prayers of praise for God's saving acts throughout history, as recorded in the Bible.
- Pray for God to grow your love for him and for the people in your life. Ask for power to follow his commands with increasing joy and diligence.
- Invite the Holy Spirit to show you where you've developed a subtle and hidden (or bold and brazen) attitude of "How far can I go?"

- Pray for power to live with an ever-growing "How faithful can I be?" attitude in all you do.

God does not use only perfect people. He can use faithful people like David. He can even use faithless people like Samson.

Between Sessions

PERSONAL REFLECTION

Take time for personal reflection, and think about the following questions …

Reflect on the first four of the Ten Commandments (Exod. 20:3–11). In which areas of your life are you doing well obeying these commandments? How can you celebrate and build on this good spiritual growth? What step of growth can you take in your relationship with God?

Reflect on the final six of the Ten Commandments (vv. 12–17). In which areas of your life are you doing well obeying these commandments? How can you celebrate and build on this good spiritual development in your relational world? What step of growth can you take in your relationships with the people God has placed in your life?

In which areas of your life are you taking the easy route and the quick payoff of disobedience? What steps can you take to start walking more diligently on the long road of obedience to the will and ways of God?

Our lives are filled with power as we keep our commitments to God. The formula for weakness is compromise.

PERSONAL PRAYER JOURNEY

Make a list of the messes you're facing in life. Then write out simple prayers surrendering these areas to God and asking for his power, wisdom, and guidance to help you overcome.

_____

_____

_____

_____

_____

_____

God wants our strength, but it's good to know that he will use even our weaknesses.

PERSONAL ACTIONS

Your Need, God's Provision

In the video, John told his story about losing much of what was precious to him and going through a messy season of pain and struggle. At the same time, he also experienced a growing awareness of God's presence and provision. Think back on two or three times in your life (recent or many years ago) when you experienced loss and pain. Write down not only how you felt but also how God provided or showed his presence in powerful ways.

My Time of Struggle and Loss:

When: _____

What I lost in this season of my life:

- _____
- _____
- _____
- _____

How God showed up and provided, was present, or revealed his amazing power:

- _____
- _____
- _____
- _____

One big spiritual lesson I learned during this time of my life:

_____

_____

_____

_____

My Time of Struggle and Loss:

When: _____

What I lost in this season of my life:

- _____

- _____

- _____

- _____

How God showed up and provided, was present, or revealed his amazing power:

- _____

- _____

- _____

- _____

One big spiritual lesson I learned during this time of my life:

_____

_____

_____

_____

My Time of Struggle and Loss:

When: _____

What I lost in this season of my life:

- _____

- _____
- _____
- _____

How God showed up and provided, was present, or revealed his amazing power:

- _____
- _____
- _____
- _____

One big spiritual lesson I learned during this time of my life:

_____

_____

_____

_____

Signs of Grace

Write out each of the Ten Commandments in your own words, expressing what you believe is the heart of each command. Then, in your own words, describe how you believe this commandment shows the grace of God to you and others.

First commandment:

_____

_____

Ways this commandment shows God's grace and goodness:

- _____

- _____

- _____

Second commandment:

_____

_____

Ways this commandment shows God's grace and goodness:

- _____

- _____

- _____

Third commandment:

_____

_____

Ways this commandment shows God's grace and goodness:

- _____

- _____

- _____

Fourth commandment:

_____

_____

Ways this commandment shows God's grace and goodness:

- _____
- _____
- _____

Fifth commandment:

_____

_____

Ways this commandment shows God's grace and goodness:

- _____
- _____
- _____

Sixth commandment:

_____

_____

Ways this commandment shows God's grace and goodness:

- _____
- _____
- _____

Seventh commandment:

_____

_____

Ways this commandment shows God's grace and goodness:

- _____

- _____

- _____

Eighth commandment:

_____

_____

Ways this commandment shows God's grace and goodness:

- _____

- _____

- _____

Ninth commandment:

_____

_____

Ways this commandment shows God's grace and goodness:

- _____

- _____

- _____

Tenth commandment:

_____

_____

Ways this commandment shows God's grace and goodness:

• _____

• _____

• _____

The Ten Commandments aren't narrow legalism but rather great love.

"The Lord Will Fight for You.... Be Quiet"

We live in a crazy, busy, messy world. Sometimes what we need most is silence, solitude, and the still waters that the Good Shepherd offers freely to his people. Try the following simple exercise two or three times each week for the next month. When you're in a tense, anxious, or messy situation, take five minutes to be still.

1. Get in a quiet place. You might go for a walk outside or find a place in your home where you can shut out the noise of life. You might even need to just go into the bathroom and close the door.

2. Open your Bible or a Bible app on your phone and read Psalm 46 slowly and reflectively.

3. Pray in three distinct ways:

• *Lord, let me find peace and trust in you.*

• *Give me wisdom to treat others with grace, even when things are tense and messy.*

• *Through the rest of my day, help me carry the peace you're giving me right now.*

If this is a helpful discipline, make it part of your normal spiritual walk of faith.

God is a rescuer, redeemer, provider, and deliverer—that is who he is.

DEEPER LEARNING

As you reflect on what God has been teaching you during this session, review chapters 6–10 of *The Good Book*.

JOURNAL, REFLECTIONS, AND NOTES

_____

_____

_____

_____

_____

_____

_____

_____

_____

_____

_____

_____

_____

_____

_____

_____

_____

_____

_____

_____

_____

_____

_____

_____

_____

SESSION 3

God Is Big

What will define you? Your problems or the God who is bigger than any of the struggles and pain this life brings? When we encounter God in the vastness of his power and glory, our eyes are opened to see that his protection, forgiveness, presence, and wisdom are always enough to overcome the problems we face.

THE BIG PICTURE

Session Title: God Is Big

The Story Line: Problems and pain come crashing into every life. Job suffered epic losses for no apparent reason. David faced the tormenting pain of his own foolish and sinful choices. In both cases, God was present and his power was great enough to carry these men through their pain and sorrow. The story of the Good Book reveals a God who is patient and present with his children in our time of deepest need. In these moments we're tempted to run from him, but the wise course of action is to run hard and fast straight into the arms of our big God.

The Time Line: Approximately 2000 BC to 1000 BC

Key Books:
- Job
- Psalms
- Proverbs

Key Themes:
- We all face hard times and are tempted to run from God.
- In the hardest times of life, we should run to God.
- God is faithful, even in our times of suffering.
- God is bigger than whatever we face, including our sin.
- Repentance is more than saying we did something wrong; it is reaffirming our love for God and choosing to follow his ways.
- To overcome the troubles we face, we need the wisdom of God.

Key Characters:
- Job
- David
- Solomon

Prayer Direction:
- Ask God to help you run to him when you face hard times.

- Pray for a deep personal understanding of God's grace when you face hard times because of your own sinful actions and choices.
- Ask the Holy Spirit to give you wisdom and clear direction to follow God in every hard and painful situation life throws at you.

INTRODUCTION

Take One … Take Two

Maria experienced a call to serve Jesus and his church. From childhood she'd been confident that one day she would be a missionary. She attended a great Christian college and was doing master's-level work to prepare for a lifetime of serving Jesus, his church, and the world. She had debt because of her school bills and worked at a local church to help make ends meet. Through all of this, Maria remained faithful and pressed on month by month. She studied, prayed, and engaged in ministry with tenacious passion.

Then, like a lightning bolt striking on a clear day, Maria's life suddenly changed. A doctor's appointment led to some extra tests and then a life-altering diagnosis. Stage 3 cancer was the verdict, but doctors assured her that with treatment and time, there was a good chance she could beat the illness.

At age twenty-seven, Maria could respond to the news and the surprising detour she's facing in any number of ways. What will she do? Will her faith stand strong as this category 5 hurricane batters the shores of her life?

Take one. Maria is angry. She has been faithful, and now it looks as if God hasn't kept up his end of the bargain. Her prayers have grown cold. Her faith has been shaken, and she's beginning to push away her Christian friends. Maria quits her church job and stops going to church. She wonders, *How can I follow a God who would let this happen to me?* Though she knows there's a good chance she'll weather this storm, she focuses on the hardships and not on the God who can carry her through them.

Take two. Maria is shocked. She didn't see this coming. Her tears flow, but her prayers grow and her faith stays intact. She rearranges her schedule to accommodate the medical treatments and the resulting side effects, but she continues serving at the church and keeping up with her studies, albeit in a reduced form. She mobilizes a team of family and friends to pray for God's comfort and healing. Maria not only allows but even invites her Christian friends to come near and support her during this time of deep personal need.

If you've walked the road of faith for very long, you've seen Jesus-loving people face significant storms in their lives. You've seen some of them draw near to God in the hard times and grow stronger in faith. Sadly, you've likely also seen some people turn from God and run away when they needed him most.

The real question is this: How will you respond when a storm hits your life?

TALK ABOUT IT

Tell about a time you faced a major storm in your life and *pulled away* from God and his people. How did this movement away from faith and fellowship affect you and the people around you?

Or

Tell about a time a major storm descended on your life and you *ran toward* God and held on to his people as a source of strength. How did this movement toward God and his people help you through the storm?

The places we go to look for help shed light on what we believe about God.

VIDEO TEACHING NOTES

Where do we turn in the hard times of life?

Rita's story

Job's journey of suffering and loss

Donny and Robyn's story

Psalm 23: Confidence in God's protection

Psalm 51: Forgiveness overcomes guilt

Psalm 139: The power of God's presence

Proverbs: The strength of wisdom

VIDEO DISCUSSION

1. When we face hard times and decide to run toward God instead of pull away from him, this can grow our faith in powerful ways. Describe a time you leaned into God because of pain, loss, or struggle. What did you learn about him that you might not have learned in any other circumstances?

> *There's something about a desperate moment that allows us to see the bigness of God.*

2. How can sharing our grief and loss with others (along with what God is teaching us through our suffering) help us and those with whom we share?

3. When storms hit our lives and the pain is intense, many people turn away from God and seek comfort or help in other things. What are some of the things people turn toward? Why don't these things ultimately satisfy or help them through the storms?

> *When we're hurting, God gives us the greatest gift he has to offer: himself!*

Read Job 1:12–22.

4. What do you learn about Job by looking at his response to all the suffering he faced? How can Job's life and faith serve as an example for us in times of deep loss and suffering?

5. In Psalm 34:18 we read, "The LORD is near the brokenhearted." The truth is, we often see God most clearly in desperate times and situations. How have you seen God show up in the hard times of life and heal broken hearts, including your own?

6. In Donny and Robyn's story, we're reminded that God's grace and forgiveness are bigger than our sin and brokenness. Describe how the grace and love of God revealed in Jesus have overcome your sin and the brokenness you've faced in your life.

God's power to forgive is stronger than your past.

7. In Robyn's story, she describes how God spoke to her and assured her that one day she would share the story of how her marriage was healed and that her story would bring hope to other people facing the same pain she experienced. How has God spoken to you in times of great desperation and pain? How did the message he spoke help you through your suffering to a place of healing?

*Times of desperation are an opportunity
to experience the power and presence
of God in profound ways.*

Read Psalm 23.

8. How have you experienced God as your good shepherd in *one* of the following ways?

- Your provider
- The one who refreshes you
- The one who guides your steps
- Your protector in hard times
- The one who comforts you
- The one who fills you to overflowing

Guilt is experiencing the full weight of our own selfishness.

Read Psalm 51:1–4, 10–15.

9. Repentance is more than just admitting we've done something wrong. It's also reaffirming our love for God and living in a way that reflects this love. How is David a powerful example of repenting in word and action?

10. If someone wronged you, said a quick "I'm sorry," and then did the same thing a couple of days later, what would you think about that person's apology and repentant attitude? What would it take for you to believe that person was truly sorry for what he or she did? How is this similar to God's desire for us to show our repentance not just with words but with actions?

Read Psalm 139:1–13.

11. What do you learn about God's presence and intimacy in your life from this passage? Which declaration in this passage strikes you the strongest, and what do you believe God is saying to you through it? Psalm 139 is a staggering picture of God's

bigness in the midst of our smallness. How does this knowledge increase your confidence and courage in a challenging world? What are some ways we can expand our understanding of how big our God is?

God's presence brings with it everything else we need!

CLOSING PRAYER

Take time as a group to pray in some of the following directions …

- Thank God that he never leaves you, no matter what this life throws at you.
- Pray for the members of your group who are in the middle of big storms right now. Ask God to show them that he is bigger than anything they're facing.
- Praise God that his power is greater than anything the Enemy tries to do in this world.
- God can heal even the most broken relationships. Pray for people you know and love who are facing relationship problems.
- Pray that each member of your group will experience God as their good shepherd.

God's presence is powerful, more powerful than any answer.

Between Sessions

PERSONAL REFLECTION

Take time for personal reflection, and think about the following questions ...

How has God shown himself to be your good shepherd? How can you respond to his leadership in your life (Ps. 23)?

What keeps you from quickly confessing your sins to God and running back to him when you find yourself wandering? What steps can you take to overcome this obstacle (Ps. 51)?

What are some of the unique ways God has made you? Spend time in prayer thanking him and taking delight in the person he is making you (Ps. 139).

Everyday decisions have a cumulative power
to produce a life of wisdom.

PERSONAL PRAYER JOURNEY

Write out a prayer of thanks for a specific time God came near and brought you through a storm.

_____

_____

_____

_____

_____

Your heavenly Father's watchfulness is an
expression of his intense love.

PERSONAL ACTIONS

I Am Your Sheep
Read Psalm 23 slowly and reflectively.

Make a list of what you learn about the Good Shepherd.

_____

_____

Make a list of what you learn about God's sheep.

_____

_____

Lift up prayers thanking God for being your good shepherd. Praise him for his protection, his provision, his discipline, and his eternal plans for your life.

Write down one way you can be a more responsive and faithful sheep as you seek to follow the Good Shepherd.

_____

_____

Commit to share this with a close Christian friend, and invite him or her to pray for you and hold you accountable for taking steps to grow in your Christian life.

Repentance, Love, and Action

In this session we learned that repentance is more than just affirming and admitting that we've done something wrong. That's just the beginning of repentance. When we truly repent, a number of things happen:

- We recognize our sin.
- We admit our sin to God, ourselves, and others.
- We affirm our love for God and commit to following him again.
- We change our behavior and attitudes to align with God's plan and will.

Monitor how you're doing with repenting and turning back to God.

Write down one area where you've wandered from God's ways and his will for your life.

_____

_____

Walk through this process and reflect honestly on your need to repent:

1. *God, I recognize this attitude or action as sin.*
2. I admit this sin to myself and God.
3. I commit to be ready to admit my sin to others who have been affected by it.
4. *God Almighty, I affirm my love for you in this specific area of my life.*
5. I will make the following changes to align my life fully and passionately with God's will for me.

Living in the Wisdom of God

God not only provides his presence but also supplies the wisdom we need to live for him in this world. God would rather have us learn his wisdom and walk in his ways than walk in our own ways and constantly need his discipline to bring us to repentance. When we walk in his wisdom, he can guide and redirect us as needed.

One of the best ways to grow in wisdom is to read the book of Proverbs, which contains practical wisdom from God for many areas of our lives. Take time in the coming days to read some of the suggested portions of Proverbs. Use the space provided to record your insights about the wisdom God gives in some very practical areas. Try to find three to five specific ways God calls us to live that reflect his wisdom in each area.

God's wisdom for how I use my words (Prov. 12:18–23; 18:17–21):

- _____
- _____
- _____
- _____
- _____

God's wisdom for how I view and use finances (8:10–21; 10:1–16):

- _____
- _____
- _____
- _____
- _____

God's wisdom for how I conduct myself in friendships and relationships (16:28; 18:21–24; 22:9–25):

- _____
- _____
- _____
- _____
- _____

God's wisdom for how I behave in my marriage (5:15–22; 31:10–31):

- _____
- _____
- _____
- _____
- _____

God's wisdom for how I view and use my sexuality (5:1–23; 6:20–7:27):

- _____
- _____
- _____
- _____
- _____

God's wisdom for how I conduct myself in business (11:1–7; 22:22–29):

- _____
- _____
- _____
- _____
- _____

God's wisdom for how I … (add your own topic and Proverbs references here):

- _____

- _____
- _____
- _____
- _____

> *Wisdom is doing the right thing at the*
> *right time for the right reasons.*

DEEPER LEARNING

As you reflect on what God has been teaching you during this session, review chapters 11–15 of *The Good Book*.

JOURNAL, REFLECTIONS, AND NOTES

_____

_____

_____

_____

_____

_____

_____

_____

_____

_____

_____

_____

_____

_____

_____

_____

_____

_____

_____

_____

_____

_____

_____

_____

_____

SESSION 4

Tough Love, Troubled Times

If you try to live out the teachings of the Bible in a consistent and committed way, you'll run into roadblocks, conflicts, and problems. The real question is not "Will I face resistance to living in obedience to the will of God?" but "How will I respond when I face strong resistance to living out my faith in this world?" The best answer to this question is "I will draw near to the God who has come close to me."

THE BIG PICTURE

Session Title: Tough Love, Troubled Times

The Story Line: The history of the Bible, God's Good Book, is filled with stories of people seeking to be faithful to God. Some fared well; others really struggled. In every case, when people were willing to try their best to follow God, he came near and helped them on their journeys. When times get tough, God comes near. When his people recognize his presence, take his hand, and follow his leading, they find strength for the journey, no matter how hard or long it might be.

The Time Line: Approximately 700 BC to 500 BC

Key Books:
- Jonah
- Isaiah
- Daniel

Key Themes:
- Those who follow God's ways will bump up against cultural norms.
- God is present when we seek to be faithful to him in a harsh world.
- Jesus is the perfect revelation of God's love and presence.
- The Bible gives us examples of people being faithful in hard times.
- We need to know the will of God and do it.

Key Characters:
- Shadrach, Meshach, and Abednego
- Jonah
- Isaiah

Prayer Direction:
- Ask God to grant you courage and strength to follow him, even when the world is walking in the opposite direction.

- Pray for a tender heart that is moved to meet the needs all around you, and ask for the power to engage in compassionate action.
- Thank God for sending Jesus to be your Savior and walk with you through every storm that comes into your life.

INTRODUCTION

Spectators or Athletes?

We live in a sports-saturated world. Channel after channel of programming is available for us to tune in and devour countless hours of football, baseball, basketball, soccer, and other conventional sports. But we can also find channels that offer plenty of unconventional competitions like Ping-Pong, darts, billiards, hot-dog eating, Frisbee catching for dogs, and even the World's Strongest Man events. The options seem endless.

As diverse as these sports and competitions might be, they all have one thing in common: only a small number of people play, but lots of people watch. We've become obsessed with watching people compete. Most of us are being passively entertained. Only a few actually do something.

Sadly, this same trend can seep into the church and our personal faith. We can be lulled into believing that listening to a preacher, attending a church, and watching religious stuff happen qualify as following Jesus. The heart of God longs to see his people get off their spiritual recliners, out of the stands, and off the sidelines. We need to get on the field and become spiritual athletes who engage in a faith that demands something and leads us to action.

TALK ABOUT IT

Give some examples of what the Christian faith can look like when we shift into spectator mode. Why is this dangerous for our spiritual health?

Or

Give some examples of what it looks like when we get on the field, take action, and become spiritually fit and active.

God honors those who
remain faithful to him.

VIDEO TEACHING NOTES

Two ways God has shown his provision for us

Sarah's story

The bold faithfulness of three young men (the book of Daniel)

Shilo's story

Jonah runs from the will of God

Isaiah paints a picture of Jesus

What faithful following can look like in our lives

VIDEO DISCUSSION

1. Tell about a time a person or situation pressured you to bend on what you knew God wants and expects. How did you respond, and what consequences did you face?

2. What have you sacrificed, or what price have you paid, because of your decision to follow Jesus faithfully?

3. How does praying in the midst of real turmoil offer insight, power, and wisdom to make it through?

Read Daniel 3:1–6, 13–23.

4. The three young men in Daniel hit a point where pagan culture collided with God's will and desire. How did they respond? What are ways we respond (for better or worse) when we bump up against cultural roadblocks and barriers?

There will be times when faithfulness to God will require sacrifice.

5. What are some of the ways you see God's will and ways bumping up against the changing norms and behaviors in our culture today? In what ways does the world pressure us to bow down and accept idolatry? How can we stand up and resist? How have you resisted? What happened?

Read Daniel 3:24–27.

6. How have you experienced the unmistakable presence of Jesus during a furnace time in your life?

7. How is your faith being tested right now? In what ways have you experienced Jesus with you during this trial?

Make every effort to ensure that you're on God's side.

Read Jonah 1:1–3.

8. In what ways do we run from God and resist his leading? How do these efforts to run from God's will and leading tend to turn out?

To run from God is not only disobedient;
it's ultimately self-destructive.

9. Jonah knew God's will for him; he just didn't want to follow God's clear leading. In which areas of your life have you learned to hear God's voice with greater clarity and follow his leading more quickly? Tell about one way you follow God's plan for your life more quickly and fully once you have clarity and a sense of what he wants you to do.

Read Isaiah 53:1–7.

10. In this passage, Isaiah painted a prophetic picture of Jesus. We see the first clear portrayal of our Savior, the One who refused to

stay in heaven and be a spectator. What do you learn about Jesus's character, life, and ministry in this prophecy?

Prophets like Isaiah remind us that God
isn't making up history as he goes.

11. How did Jesus show us the way of humble service as he left heaven, came to this earth, lived as a man, and sacrificed himself for us? In the video we heard the story of Shilo and her LOVE Lunchsack Ministry. What are some ways you can engage in humble service in the name of Jesus?

12. Where is God calling you to take a stand for him, and how have you responded to this call? What next step do you need to take to be fully faithful to his call?

God's commands, not personal qualifications,
determine how to spend our lives in his service.

CLOSING PRAYER

Take time as a group to pray in some of the following directions ...

- Thank God for being with you in the easy times and the hard times of life. Pray that you'll grow in your awareness of his presence.

- Ask God not only for eyes to see when you're being tempted to compromise but also for his strength to resist and overcome temptation.
- Pray for God to grow humility in you that reflects the humble heart of Jesus. Ask for eyes to see real needs that you can humbly meet in the name of Jesus.
- Ask God to keep you from running away from hard situations and teach you instead to run toward challenges that will honor him.
- Lift up praise that Jesus willingly and gladly went to the cross for you and all those who receive and walk in his grace.

The presence of Jesus emboldens us to follow him faithfully.

Between Sessions

PERSONAL REFLECTION

Take time for personal reflection, and think about the following questions …

How have you experienced the presence of God in hard times? In what ways has he shown up, comforted you, and provided for your needs?

What specific sacrifice do you feel you need to make but haven't yet acted on? What can you do to live in greater submission to God in this area of your life?

Are you more like Jonah or Jesus? How can you be more like your Savior?

Our character becomes credible as we move
from selfishness to selflessness.

PERSONAL PRAYER JOURNEY

Write prayers asking God to make you more of a spiritual athlete and less of a spiritual spectator.

_____

_____

_____

_____

_____

Write prayers for your local church leaders to be bold in standing for what is true and right and to never compromise on the Word of God.

_____

_____

_____

_____

_____

The challenge is to be Jesus followers who fully
reflect the character of our Savior.

PERSONAL ACTIONS

Culture Collision

Make a list of four to six areas in which you see culture colliding with what God says he wants people to experience to truly flourish. These can be small and seemingly insignificant collisions or big and obvious ones. These are things you know are opposed to God's Word and will but seem to be more and more common in our world and culture. In each case, write a few words about the specific actions, attitudes, and lifestyles our culture is promoting. Then next to these words, write what God's heart and will are for his people.

- _____
- _____
- _____
- _____
- _____
- _____

Identify one area where you see yourself sliding away from God's will and toward the ways of the world. In the space below, describe the challenge you're facing.

_____

_____

Write out some of the negative consequences you might experience (or are already experiencing) if you continue down this road and let this pattern of poor choices persist in your life.

- _____
- _____
- _____
- _____

Set one or two specific goals you want to act on that will reverse this trend and move you toward living more in line with God's will in this area of your life.

_____

_____

_____

Finally, write the name of the person you'll invite to pray for you and hold you accountable to work on growing in this area of your life. Also write down when you'll call or connect with this person and ask for support. (Do this face-to-face or voice to voice, not by text or email. This will make room for some authentic and meaningful conversation and hopefully a time to pray together.)

_____

_____

_____

Obedience to God requires great effort, especially when we find ourselves moving against the flow of comfort and convenience.

A Study in Contrasts

Read Daniel 3, and then list the characteristics and actions that marked the lives of Daniel's three friends Hananiah, Azariah, and Mishael. Be specific about what they did and what seemed to motivate them.

- _____

- _____

- _____

Next, read Jonah 1 and make a list of Jonah's actions and attitudes. Also note what seemed to motivate him to run from God's call.

- _____
- _____
- _____

List two or three clear contrasts between how the three men and Jonah responded to challenging times.

_____

_____

_____

Describe one challenge you're facing in your life right now.

_____

_____

What steps can you take to live more like Daniel's three friends and less like Jonah? What attitudes and actions should mark your life?

_____

_____

_____

Getting in the Game

Make a choice to get off the sidelines and into the game. In the coming week, set up a meeting with a leader at your church who can help you discover your spiritual gifts and find a place to serve Jesus, his church, and those who don't yet know the love of God.

Which church leader will you call? When will you contact this person?

Pray for a humble heart that is ready to learn from this leader, and be open to engage in a new journey of serving Jesus and others.

Humble are those who consistently take inventory
of their motives and means of success.

DEEPER LEARNING

As you reflect on what God has been teaching you during this session, review chapters 16–20 of *The Good Book*.

JOURNAL, REFLECTIONS, AND NOTES

_____

_____

_____

_____

_____

_____

_____

_____

_____

_____

_____

_____

_____

_____

_____

_____

_____

_____

_____

_____

_____

_____

_____

_____

_____

Jesus Has Just Entered the Building

Jesus is closer than we realize. He didn't stay aloof in heaven and give us a list of spiritual dos and don'ts. Instead, he came among us, as one of us. While maintaining his full divinity, Jesus took on humanity. He was born humbly in a manger, he spoke powerfully on a hillside (and many other places), he loved perfectly, and he died on a rugged Roman cross to pay for our sins. Then after three days, he rose again in power and glory. When we see Jesus, know him, and receive his grace, we're changed. We desire to give, sacrifice, and serve in his glorious name.

THE BIG PICTURE

Session Title: Jesus Has Just Entered the Building

The Story Line: The Older Testament reveals the love of God and the brokenness of the human race. All throughout the Good Book, we discover that God knows our sins and still loves us. The culmination of his saving plan in the Bible is revealed at the very beginning of the New Testament. In four distinct and vivid accounts (Matthew, Mark, Luke, and John), we hear the story of God's humble entrance into human history. Jesus is Immanuel, God with us. He is fully human and yet fully divine. When he came to this earth, he presented himself as the perfect sacrifice to offer us new life, cleansing, and a reconciled relationship with our heavenly Father. He also offered wise teaching and the gift of the Holy Spirit to help us live for him and not for ourselves.

The Time Line: 5 BC (the birth of Jesus) through AD 30

Key Books:
- Matthew
- Luke
- John

Key Themes:
- Jesus came near us through the incarnation.
- Jesus was fully man and fully God.
- The example of Jesus's radical sacrifice can lead us to make surprising sacrifices in his name.
- Jesus died and rose again in glory.
- We're called to follow the teachings of Jesus in the power of the Holy Spirit.

Key Character:
- Jesus

Prayer Direction:

- Pray for insight to understand the greatness of who Jesus is as fully divine and fully human. Pray for humility to recognize that your mind can't entirely grasp the vastness of Jesus's divine and human natures.
- Ask God to prepare you to serve more and more like Jesus.
- Ask the Holy Spirit to enable you to live out and practice the teachings of Jesus.

INTRODUCTION

Information and Transformation

The Christian faith is more than the simple accumulation of information. It's a life of transformation. Information and transformation aren't in opposition. They are two sides of the same spiritual coin. When we know the truth and have the information God has revealed in his Good Book, every aspect of our lives can be transformed.

Our journey of faith in Christ begins with information. God has spoken, revealed his truth, and given us his Word, the Bible. This Holy Book gives us information about God's love, our sin, the incarnation of Jesus, the death of our Savior, the glory of the resurrection, and so much more. Without the right information, we can't experience lasting transformation. We must know God's Word, accept it as true, and become mature in our thinking. But this is only the beginning of the journey.

Right belief and acceptance of biblical teaching should always lead to a transformed life. Jesus taught us about how to love God, others in the family of faith, and even those who don't yet know the good news of salvation. Our Lord modeled humility and service so we can follow his example as the Spirit enables us. The life of Jesus not only shapes our thinking but also orders our steps and influences our daily choices.

Information without any life change can become a game of Bible trivia. It can lead to pride about our great knowledge, but not a life like Jesus's. On the other hand, transformation without solid biblical information can send us racing down the road in the wrong direction. We can be sincere, but sincerely wrong.

When we read the Gospels—the four amazing accounts of the life of Jesus in Matthew, Mark, Luke, and John—we gain all the information we need to embrace Jesus as the divine Son of God. We also learn that he is the humble one who came in a manger and died on a cross for us. While we're learning this, the Holy Spirit moves us to action. We grow in a passion to fully yield our lives to the Savior, to follow his ways, and to live for him. This beautiful merging of true biblical teaching (orthodoxy) and lasting life transformation (orthopraxy) leads to a life of spiritual health and joy.

TALK ABOUT IT

What are some of the consequences for people who seem deeply committed to knowing the right Bible information but don't let the truth change how they conduct themselves in their daily lives?

Or

Tell about a person (no name necessary) you observed who was zealous to live for Jesus but didn't take time to dig into the Bible and learn the truth. What are some of the potential dangers of this imbalanced approach to faith?

Because Jesus was fully God, he is the only one
who can become our perfect sacrifice.

VIDEO TEACHING NOTES

A core truth of our faith

Greg's story

The incarnation … God comes near us

True love leads to deep sacrifice

Diane's story

The message on the mount

The power of practice

VIDEO DISCUSSION

1. Tell about a time you saw a Christian sacrifice in a way that was costly and demanded a deep commitment to Jesus. Why do you think this person made such a surprising sacrifice?

Read Philippians 2:5–8.

2. In your own words, express what Jesus sacrificed to

- leave the glory of heaven;
- take on human flesh and become one of us; and
- be crucified on the cross and take our pain, shame, and judgment.

We're on the receiving end of the greatest sacrifice of all time.

3. In Greg's story, he talks about what-if moments that cause us to hit the brakes and not follow God's leading. What causes you to pull back and not fully surrender your life to Jesus? If applicable, tell about a what-if moment you are facing today. How can group members pray for you as you seek to move forward with a surrendered heart?

4. For Greg to truly give (in his case, a kidney), someone had to willingly accept the gift. Tell about a time someone offered something to you (big or small) and you joyfully accepted the gift? How did you feel, and how do you think the person felt?

5. How do you think Jesus feels when someone accepts the gift of his life and his great sacrifice on the cross? How do you think he feels when someone refuses the gift and sacrifice he has offered?

*God's grace doesn't merely offer to make us
better; it promises to make us new.*

6. Tell about a time you gave something sacrificially. Describe how it made you feel when someone else benefited and was blessed by your gift.

7. What would selfless sacrifice look like if you decided to follow Jesus's example in *one* of the following places:

- Your home
- Your workplace
- Your neighborhood
- Your church
- Your extended family
- Your community
- Some other place God has put you

The depth of love can be determined by the level of sacrifice.

Read Isaiah 7:14 and Matthew 1:22–23.

8. If you really understood and embraced the truth that Jesus was and is Immanuel (God with us), how might this affect the way you face challenges and problems in your daily life? How has knowing Jesus as Immanuel helped you battle fear, anxiety, or worry?

9. Jesus entered history as a vulnerable baby in radically humble circumstances. What message do you think he was and is seeking to give us? In what unique ways does the incarnation of Jesus reveal God's love for us?

*Grace reconciles our past with forgiveness and
empowers our future with hope.*

10. How have you noticed God seeking to shape you into his image through recent experiences in your life? In what ways are you changing as a person and becoming more like Jesus?

Read Matthew 5:13–16.
11. Jesus calls us to believe certain truths. But these truths are also meant to change our actions and daily lives. We're called to practice specific behaviors, attitudes, and actions that reflect the truth Jesus has taught us. In these words from the message on the mount, what is Jesus calling us to do that will bring him glory and joy? What are specific ways you can shine the light of Jesus in the places he sends you in a normal week?

Jesus is the pattern God uses to shape his people.

Read Matthew 6:5–15.
12. What specific lessons does Jesus teach us about prayer? How should we pray, and what should we be praying about? What is one

specific prayer lesson from Jesus that you need to adopt more fully and actively in your life?

Prayer is not only speaking to God; it's also listening to him.

CLOSING PRAYER

Take time as a group to pray in some of the following directions ...

- Praise God for his ultimate act of humility in coming down from heaven to be with us.
- Ask the Holy Spirit to stir you to actions of humility as you interact with others.
- Pray for courage to sacrifice boldly for the sake of others.
- Invite the Holy Spirit to sensitize your heart to a sacrifice God wants you to make as you follow Jesus on an adventure of obedience.
- Ask God to help you grow as a person of passionate and sincere prayer.
- Confess your tendency to be judgmental, and ask God to humble your heart and grow your ability to forgive and extend grace.

Let it be your ambition to have greater boldness in your life.

Between Sessions

PERSONAL REFLECTION

Take time for personal reflection, and think about the following questions …

How can you share the message and love of Jesus with people who aren't yet aware of his love for them? What specific people do you need to begin praying for?

How does your prayer life reflect Jesus's teaching in Matthew 6:5–15? How can you deepen your prayer life?

Based on Jesus's teaching in Matthew 7:1–6, in what ways do you tend to judge others? What steps can you take to overcome this tendency? How can you extend greater grace to others?

Jesus often uses the weakest, most difficult areas
of our lives to mold us into his likeness.

PERSONAL PRAYER JOURNEY

Journal prayers of thanks for how Jesus surrendered, sacrificed, and gave himself for you.

_____

_____

_____

Write prayers of devotion to live a more sacrificial life for Jesus.

_____

_____

_____

Jesus is fully human; in him we have the perfect model for humanity.

PERSONAL ACTIONS

The Message on the Mount

Read Matthew 5–7 and study some of the specific practices Jesus taught his disciples. Then list the lessons you're learning from this message and some actions you can take to live out the practices Jesus talked about.

_____

_____

_____

_____

Read each of the following passages and write your reflections and commitments in the space provided.

Read Matthew 5:21–26.

Main message:

_____

_____

Lessons I'm learning:

- _____

- _____

- _____

Actions I need to take:

- _____

- _____

Read Matthew 5:27–30.

Main message:

_____

_____

Lessons I'm learning:

- _____

- _____

- _____

Actions I need to take:

- _____

- _____

Read Matthew 5:43–48.

Main message:

_____

_____

Lessons I'm learning:

- _____

- _____

- _____

Actions I need to take:

- _____

- _____

Read Matthew 6:1–4.

Main message:

_____

_____

Lessons I'm learning:

- _____

- _____

- _____

Actions I need to take:

- _____
- _____

Read Matthew 6:19–24.

Main message:

_____

_____

Lessons I'm learning:

- _____
- _____
- _____

Actions I need to take:

- _____
- _____

Read Matthew 7:1–6.

Main message:

_____

_____

Lessons I'm learning:

- _____
- _____
- _____

Actions I need to take:

- _____

- _____

Because Jesus is divine, he can speak
with authority into our lives.

Surprising Blessings

Jesus taught a lot about the pathway to blessedness (true, lasting, and deep happiness). Take time to reflect on each of the qualities Jesus described, and ask yourself how you can grow this characteristic in your heart and life.

Read Matthew 5:3–12.

"Blessed are the poor in spirit, for the kingdom of heaven is theirs"
(v. 3).

What was Jesus saying? What should this quality look like in my heart and life?

_____

_____

What is one way I can deepen this trait in my heart and life?

_____

_____

"Blessed are those who mourn, for they will be comforted" (v. 4).

What was Jesus saying? What should this quality look like in my heart and life?

_____

_____

What is one way I can deepen this trait in my heart and life?

_____

_____

"Blessed are the humble, for they will inherit the earth" (v. 5).

What was Jesus saying? What should this quality look like in my heart and life?

_____

_____

What is one way I can deepen this trait in my heart and life?

_____

_____

"Blessed are those who hunger and thirst for righteousness, for they will be filled" (v. 6).

What was Jesus saying? What should this quality look like in my heart and life?

_____

_____

What is one way I can deepen this trait in my heart and life?

_____

_____

"Blessed are the merciful, for they will be shown mercy" (v. 7).

What was Jesus saying? What should this quality look like in my heart and life?

_____

_____

_____

What is one way I can deepen this trait in my heart and life?

_____

_____

"Blessed are the pure in heart, for they will see God" (v. 8).

What was Jesus saying? What should this quality look like in my heart and life?

_____

_____

What is one way I can deepen this trait in my heart and life?

_____

_____

"Blessed are the peacemakers, for they will be called sons of God" *(v. 9).*

What was Jesus saying? What should this quality look like in my heart and life?

_____

_____

What is one way I can deepen this trait in my heart and life?

_____

_____

"Blessed are those who are persecuted because of righteousness, for the kingdom of heaven is theirs" (v. 10).

What was Jesus saying? What should this quality look like in my heart and life?

_____

_____

What is one way I can deepen this trait in my heart and life?

_____

_____

"You are blessed when [people] insult you and persecute you and falsely say every kind of evil against you because of me. Be glad and

rejoice, because your reward is great in heaven. For that is how they persecuted the prophets who were before you" (vv. 11–12).

What was Jesus saying? What should this quality look like in my heart and life?

_____

_____

What is one way I can deepen this trait in my heart and life?

_____

_____

> *Genuine spirituality longs for the approval*
> *of God, not the applause of people.*

Standing Strong in the Storms
Read Matthew 7:24–27.

List the ways you're actively and intentionally building your life on the solid rock of Jesus Christ (his teachings, his ways, your relationship with him).

- _____
- _____
- _____
- _____

List the ways you're building your life on other foundations that just might be shifting sand.

- _____
- _____
- _____
- _____

What specific steps can you take to stop building your life on an unsound foundation? You might want to invite one or two trusted Christian friends to pray for you and encourage you as you make these foundational life shifts.

- _____
- _____
- _____
- _____

We follow and practice the teachings of Jesus in the good times so we're prepared for the hard times.

DEEPER LEARNING

As you reflect on what God has been teaching you during this session, review chapters 21–25 of *The Good Book*.

JOURNAL, REFLECTIONS, AND NOTES

SESSION 6

Jesus Won't Leave Us as We Are

The world is broken, sin is poisoning homes and nations, and many people don't seem to notice or care. How does God respond to the desperate condition of humanity? He comes running toward us, arms wide open, ready to save, cleanse, and bring us home. What a staggering spiritual reality. God doesn't leave us where we are! We're steeped in sin; he offers cleansing. We are broken; he offers healing. We're mired in the pain of this world; he is preparing a place in heaven for us to be with him. This is good news!

THE BIG PICTURE

Session Title: Jesus Won't Leave Us as We Are

The Story Line: Sin raised its ugly head all the way back in the first book of the Bible. Adam and Eve rebelled against God, and the universe began to spin out of control. Brokenness became the norm. Yet God never settled for a world on the verge of disaster. Instead, he came among us—Jesus, Immanuel. When Jesus bore our sins on the cross, he made a way for us to come home. When he rose from the grave in victory, he invited us to live in his resurrection glory and power every day of our lives, and forever.

The Time Line: 5 BC (the birth of Jesus) through AD 30

Key Books:
- Matthew
- Mark
- Luke
- John

Key Themes:
- Jesus is the exclusive pathway to a relationship with God.
- There is no place we can go and nothing we can do that will push us beyond the bounds of God's love and grace.
- Jesus's life, death, and resurrection are the path to our salvation.
- The resurrection of Jesus gives us hope for an eternity with the Father and the power to change today.

Key Character:
- Jesus

Prayer Direction:

- Ask Jesus to show up in the most broken and forgotten places in your community.
- Pray for eyes to see the powerful presence of the resurrected Lord Jesus in the flow of your ordinary days.
- Thank Jesus that he has made a way for us to come home to the Father.

INTRODUCTION

Broken beyond Repair?

Daniel's father sent him a couple of blocks away from home to pick up a wooden mantel clock that a skilled craftsman in their small town had repaired. Daniel's family had plenty of digital clocks around the house that kept perfect time, but this beautiful piece of craftsmanship had been in their family for generations. It was of great value to them and had a prominent place on the mantel above the fireplace.

Daniel was old enough to know better. He should have picked up the clock and walked carefully straight home. Instead, he saw some friends playing baseball in the local park and stopped to watch … then play. While having a blast with his friends, he forgot about the clock on the bench just outside the baseball diamond. He didn't think about it until, out of the corner of his eye, he saw a kid holding up a medium-sized box. Before Daniel could say a word, the box slipped out of the boy's hands and fell to the ground.

Daniel's body froze as his heart raced. He could hear shattering glass and fracturing wood. He ran to pick up the box, and when he opened it, he discovered that the situation was worse than he had expected. Shards of glass were everywhere. The body of the clock was broken. The magnitude of the situation hit Daniel, and tears began to flow.

Options ran through his mind. *Do I run away from home? Do I run home and just tell the truth? Do I make up a story and try to cover my tracks?* The clock was beyond repair, and the situation looked hopeless. Finally, from the back of his fear-clouded mind came an idea. He wouldn't run away from home or even to his home. He would take the clock to the only one who could put the pieces back together. Daniel held the box close to his chest and ran back to the clock-repair shop. When he showed the craftsman the broken clock, the man didn't get angry, yell, or scold Daniel. Instead, with a kind smile, he said, "I can fix this!" And he did.

TALK ABOUT IT

Tell about a time you broke something (an object, a relationship, or something else) you thought was beyond repair but then discovered it could be repaired.

Or

Tell about a time you watched God bring about spiritual repair, healing, or transformation in a situation you thought was hopeless.

*Remember that our challenge is to ask and then trust
that Jesus will answer in the best way possible.*

VIDEO TEACHING NOTES

Jesus's life, death, and resurrection open the way
to a restored relationship with God

Michael's story

The love of God tracks us down

Karen's story

The hope of God no matter what we face

Core beliefs of the Christian faith:

- The crucifixion of Jesus
- The death of Jesus
- The resurrection of Jesus

The why and the who in our suffering

The glorious hope of the resurrection

VIDEO DISCUSSION

1. The focus of this session is embracing the biblical declaration
that Jesus is the only way to a whole and healed relationship with
God. People today have a hard time with this, and they want to
embrace many ways, or any other way, to God. But there is no
other way! What are some of the ways people push back against
the idea that Jesus is the only way to salvation? Why do you think
there is so much resistance to this declaration of Jesus?

*Nothing pleases God more than bringing people
into a right relationship with him.*

2. In Michael's story, we see him hiding in the woods from the police, fearful and questioning his life decisions. He had hit rock bottom. Tell about a time you hit bottom and finally looked up and cried out to God. How did God respond to your cry for help?

*Sometimes we think God is chasing us down to punish us, but
then we discover that he is seeking to love and embrace us.*

3. Michael was a man who hated and antagonized Christians. But when he finally met some Christians face-to-face and gave them a chance to be themselves, he found they were caring, kind, and compassionate. What are some of the negative ways people in our culture view Christians? How can we break down those false stereotypes and help them see that we're just regular people who happen to love Jesus?

4. How have the people in God's family, the church, embraced and loved you? How can we, the people of God, do a better job of embracing and loving people who are hurting, different, or even just plain difficult?

Read Mark 10:45, Luke 15:3–7, and Luke 19:10.
5. As you look back on your life, how did God search for you, reach out to you, and bring you to himself (even if you didn't

recognize it at the time)? How does it feel to know that God loved you enough to pursue you even when you had no interest in him?

Ultimately, Jesus came to rescue and save us.

Read Luke 15:3–32.

6. Each of the three stories Jesus told in Luke 15 ended with finding what was lost. Then there was a celebration. How does God feel when a person who is lost in sin and far from him comes home and receives the grace of Jesus? How should we feel when this happens?

God is a God who is always searching for us and
is forever ready to receive us home with joy.

7. Jesus was clear that no person is beyond the love and grace of God. Think of one person in your life who seems far from God. How have you been praying for this person and reaching out to him or her? How can group members pray with you and encourage you to boldly share the story and love of Jesus with this person?

God offers a new beginning to anyone, anywhere, at any moment.

8. Karen shared her story of long-term struggle, pain, bad news, and tenacious trust in God. She was deeply committed to love, trust, and follow God even if she lost Jaren, her "miracle baby," to cancer. In what ways are we tempted to walk away from God in the

deeply painful times of life? Why is it so important that we hold on to him even tighter during these times?

Read Psalm 22:1–2 and Mark 15:33–34.

9. Jesus cried out in pain and asked his Father "Why?" as he hung on the cross bearing our sin and shame. Through Jesus's example we learn that we don't always get an answer to our whys, but God promises to always be near us in our pain. How have you personally experienced the presence of Jesus in times when things didn't make sense? How did the who become more important than the why?

> *The wounds on Jesus's hands, feet, head, and side showed the extent of God's great love for humanity.*

Read Matthew 28:16–20.

10. When Jesus rose from the dead, it was the beginning of the story, not the end. Jesus promises that we'll be with him in heaven forever, but he also gives us a mission and purpose for this life. What mission did Jesus give his followers before he returned to heaven and the Father? What are some ways we can enter more fully and enthusiastically into this mission?

> *The resurrection of Jesus changes everything.*

11. When Jesus rose from the dead, we were set free from fear. How can fully embracing the resurrection of Jesus release us from

fear today, in the future, and forever? What fear are you facing right now? How can group members pray for you to overcome this fear and walk in bold confidence because Jesus Christ is risen?

12. The resurrection of Jesus should fill our hearts and lives with joy. What one aspect of your life is lacking joy? How can focusing on the resurrection of Jesus transform how you see this part of your life?

In the resurrection of Jesus, we're given a task to
go into all the world and tell his story.

CLOSING PRAYER

Take time as a group to pray in some of the following directions …

- Ask God to bring healing and hope to our broken world.
- Thank God that he never stopped pursuing you, even when you ran from him.
- Pray together for people you love who are still wandering far from Jesus.
- Lift up people you know who love Jesus and are going through a time of great pain and struggle. Ask God to help them run to him and not away from him.
- Thank Jesus for the glory of his resurrection, and ask him to help you live in his resurrection power every day of your life.

*Unless a request requires God to contradict
either his character or his commands,
the Bible gives us permission to ask for
whatever we want in any situation.*

Between Sessions

PERSONAL REFLECTION

Take time for personal reflection, and think about the following questions …

How has God changed your heart and life in the past year? Take a moment to thank him for this.

In what specific ways did God pursue you when you were still running from him? Spend a few moments in prayer, thanking him for his relentless and seeking love.

When hard times hit, do you tend to ask the why questions or focus on the reality that God is with you? How can you focus more on the who when you encounter hard times in life?

The future of every true Christ follower is firmly in the hands of God.

PERSONAL PRAYER JOURNEY

Write prayers of praise that begin with "Because Jesus is risen from the dead, I …"

_____

_____

_____

_____

_____

> *No matter your current circumstances, all of*
> *life is infused with an eternal hope.*

PERSONAL ACTIONS

The Apostles' Creed

Read the Apostles' Creed a number of times slowly and reflectively. This is one of the ecumenical creeds that Christians all over the world declare.

> I believe in God, the Father almighty, creator of heaven and earth. I believe in Jesus Christ, God's only Son, our Lord, who was conceived by the Holy Spirit, born of the Virgin Mary, suffered under Pontius Pilate, was crucified, died, and was buried; he descended to the dead. On the third day he rose again; he ascended into heaven, he is seated

at the right hand of the Father, and he will come to judge the living and the dead. I believe in the Holy Spirit, the holy catholic church, the communion of saints, the forgiveness of sins, the resurrection of the body, and the life everlasting. Amen.

Meditate on five primary declarations in the creed that strike you, and write down what each one expresses about your faith. Then discuss an action or direction it prompts you toward.

1. Declaration in the Apostles' Creed:

_____

What this expresses about my faith:

_____

_____

How might this belief lead me to action or direct me in prayer?

_____

_____

2. Declaration in the Apostles' Creed:

_____

What this expresses about my faith:

_____

_____

How might this belief lead me to action or direct me in prayer?

_____

_____

3. Declaration in the Apostles' Creed:

_____

What this expresses about my faith:

_____

_____

How might this belief lead me to action or direct me in prayer?

_____

_____

4. Declaration in the Apostles' Creed:

_____

What this expresses about my faith:

_____

_____

_____

How might this belief lead me to action or direct me in prayer?

_____

_____

5. Declaration in the Apostles' Creed:

_____

What this expresses about my faith:

_____

_____

How might this belief lead me to action or direct me in prayer?

_____

_____

The Words of Jesus from the Cross

Read and reflect on each of the declarations Jesus made as he was hanging on the cross and dying for your sins. Then write down what you learn about Jesus, and even about yourself, in each declaration.

"Jesus said, 'Father, forgive them, because they do not know what they are doing'" (Luke 23:34).

_____

_____

_____

"[Jesus] said to [the thief on the cross], 'Truly I tell you, today you will be with me in paradise'" (v. 43).

_____

_____

_____

"When Jesus saw his mother and the disciple he loved standing there, he said to his mother, 'Woman, here is your son.' Then he said to the disciple, 'Here is your mother.' And from that hour the disciple took her into his home" (John 19:26–27).

"About three in the afternoon Jesus cried out with a loud voice, 'Elí, Elí, lemá sabachtháni?' that is, 'My God, my God, why have you abandoned me?'" (Matt. 27:46).

"When Jesus knew that everything was now finished that the Scripture might be fulfilled, he said, 'I'm thirsty'" (John 19:28).

"When Jesus had received the sour wine, he said, 'It is finished.' Then bowing his head, he gave up his spirit" (John 19:30).

"Jesus called out with a loud voice, 'Father, into your hands I entrust my spirit.' Saying this, he breathed his last" (Luke 23:46).

_____

_____

_____

On the cross Jesus shared in our pain. Whatever else death is, because of the cross we now know we no longer face it alone.

Meditate on the Resurrection
Read Luke 24 and John 20–21.

Reflect on how a firm confidence in the resurrection can affect the following three areas of your life:

1. Fear. How does the resurrection of Jesus drive fear out of your heart and life?

_____

_____

_____

2. Hope. How does the resurrection of Jesus give you hope in the circumstances of your life that feel hopeless?

_____

_____

_____

3. Meaning. How does the truth of the resurrection give meaning and purpose to your life?

_____

_____

_____

Because Christ is risen, we'll also rise.

DEEPER LEARNING

As you reflect on what God has been teaching you during this session, review chapters 26–30 of *The Good Book*.

JOURNAL, REFLECTIONS, AND NOTES

SESSION 7

Following Jesus

"Follow me!" People heard Jesus say this over and over when he walked on this planet, and he still extends this invitation to us today. It's the supreme call of the Christian faith. Jesus calls all kinds of people to follow him—surprising people, shy people, people who look good, and people who don't look good at all. When Jesus calls and someone follows, a whole new life begins.

THE BIG PICTURE

Session Title: Following Jesus

The Story Line: After the resurrection of Jesus, a new chapter in the work of God began. The church was born, and God's call on his people expanded. It became a missionary call to follow Jesus and share the life-changing message of salvation. The Holy Spirit came on the church in power and began to do two distinct things. First, more and more people were drawn to the Savior. Jews and Gentiles, slaves and free people, men and women, religious and irreligious—people from every walk of life put their faith in Jesus as the Messiah and Savior of the world. Second, once these people knew the love and grace of God, they responded to the call to move out from where they were to share this amazing good news to the ends of the earth. This part of the story of God's people is still being written today.

The Time Line: Around AD 30 (the resurrection of Jesus) to AD 63

Key Book:
- Acts

Key Themes:
- The Holy Spirit comes on believers and begins his work in and through them.
- God loves and calls all sorts of people.
- Hope is found in Jesus, even when everything seems hopeless.
- When we live together in biblical community, we show what the church should look like.
- God breaks down all sorts of barriers and divisions and binds people together in his church.

Key Characters:
- Paul
- Ananias
- Peter
- Cornelius

Prayer Direction:
- Ask the Holy Spirit to move in and through you in increasing power.
- Pray for strength to do your part as a healthy part of Christ's church.
- Confess where you allow divisions and prejudice to exist in your heart and life.

INTRODUCTION

Welcome to the Church

Shelly was born into a good Christian family and went to church on Sunday morning and Sunday evening, and for Wednesday-evening classes. She loved it. She also respected her pastor and admired his wife. Her parents were sincere about their faith and lived it out at home and in their community. The only time Shelly got in trouble at church was when it was time to go home, and her parents had to search for her and coax her to leave.

Martin grew up in a churchgoing family. He never really enjoyed attending church, but he went as long as his parents forced the issue. He struggled because the things he heard at church seemed like good ideas but he didn't see them lived out at home or anywhere else in his life. Eventually his family's church attendance tapered off and then stopped altogether, and that was fine with Martin.

Ashleigh gets sick to her stomach and nervous when she hears people talk about church. Her years in church as a young girl were dark and painful. She not only felt rejected by the other kids, but the "special" attention her youth leader showed her eventually turned into inappropriate behavior that she felt powerless to resist. For Ashleigh, God and church are bound up in one twisted, painful ball of hurt.

Kenneth grew up with no church and no real awareness of what happens in church. The truth is, he had no interest in church and no drive to figure it out. It simply wasn't on his radar. When he became a Christian and began following Jesus, he jumped into a local church. From the first day, the warmth of the people shocked him, their kindness amazed him, and their genuine joy inspired him. With the passing months and years, he fell more in love with Jesus and his people. He loved his church. So whenever Kenneth heard Christian friends complain about church stuff, he was baffled. The wonder and joy of being with God's people to sing, pray, learn, grow, and be inspired to live more for Jesus continued to amaze him.

Every person has a different experience with the church, but everyone who follows Jesus should grow to love it over time. When it comes right down to it, the church is God's people, and God wants us to love one another.

TALK ABOUT IT

Tell about your experience with church as you grew up. What was good and wonderful? What was troubling or painful?

Or

If you didn't grow up in the church, what was your impression looking in from the outside? Once you entered the church, what did you experience and discover about it?

The church isn't a building we go to;
it's a community we belong to.

VIDEO TEACHING NOTES

The Holy Spirit is at work in the church and in our personal lives

Crystal's story

The work of the Holy Spirit

The Holy Spirit gives life and power to the church

The day of Pentecost

What characteristics marked the early church

Vonda's story

The world at the time of the church's birth (and our world today)

Four biblical stories of God's holy interruptions:

- God interrupts the hyperreligious
- God interrupts a quiet life
- God interrupts a faithful life
- God interrupts a good person

God wants to break down the walls that divide us

VIDEO DISCUSSION

1. When you think about the Holy Spirit showing up and working in a person's life, what comes to mind? When people say, "I'm filled with the Spirit" or "I'm Spirit led," what do you think they mean?

The disciples who started the early church were uneducated and under-resourced. They had no strategic plan or special powers. But the Holy Spirit empowered them.

Read 2 Corinthians 1:3–5.

2. Tell about a time God helped you navigate a very difficult storm in your life and afterward you were able to encourage or help someone who was experiencing the same kind of storm.

Read Acts 1:7–8.

3. Jesus assured the disciples that they would receive power when the Holy Spirit came on them. He went on to say they would become his witnesses to the very ends of the earth. Often, when we think of missions work, faraway places come to mind. What are some of the opportunities you see in a typical week to spread the love and message of Jesus right where you are? Think of one person you feel led to reach out to. How can group members challenge you and hold you accountable to reach out to this person?

The church is a Spirit-empowered community centered around Jesus and committed to one another as we live out our faith every day.

Read John 16:5–15.

4. What does Jesus say the Holy Spirit will do when he descends on the church and enters a believer's life? How have you experienced the Spirit of God working in your life in one of these ways?

God's ultimate gift to the church was the Holy Spirit.

Read Acts 2:42–47.

5. What specific characteristics marked the community life of the first-century church? How can we embrace and grow these same practices in the life of the church today?

The teaching of the early church focused not only
on simply downloading information but also on
leading people to life transformation.

6. Vonda tells the story of how God interrupted her life and led her in a very different direction from what she would have expected or planned. Tell a story about a time God led you in a direction you didn't expect and wouldn't have planned. How has your faith grown because of this?

God will never command anything
contrary to what he has already
revealed through Scripture.

Read Acts 9:1–16.

7. How did God show up in Saul's life, transform him, and give him a new direction? Tell the story of how God showed up in your life and drew you to himself. How has the course of your life been changed because you were willing to follow God's will and not your own plan?

8. Think of someone you know (or know about) who seems beyond the hope of real change. How can you look at this person in a fresh, new way and see hope and potential for transformation in his or her life? How can you pray for this person with new passion and faith-filled hope?

> *When God interrupts our lives, it's often an*
> *invitation to do something uncomfortable.*

Read Acts 9:13–19.

9. What do you learn about the character and faith of Ananias in this account? How does his example inspire you to take risks as you follow Jesus? What is one risk you've resisted taking?

Read Acts 10.

10. What was the religious and cultural background of Cornelius? How did God call him? What was God teaching Peter through this encounter?

> *God's love reconciles people to one another.*

11. Prejudice and discrimination are nothing new. But it's especially sad when these attitudes exist in the hearts and lives of Jesus followers. What were some of the prejudices Peter dealt with, and how did God change his heart and lifestyle?

12. What are some of the attitudes and behaviors (that are really veiled forms of racism, prejudice, or discrimination) that can exist in the hearts of Christians? What are some ways we can battle these attitudes, call them what they are, and repent of them?

God's love can bridge the deepest divides.

CLOSING PRAYER

Take time as a group to pray in some of the following directions …

- Thank God that he is with you and in you through the presence and power of the Holy Spirit.
- Give God thanks for the people he has placed in your life who have extended the grace of Jesus to you in hard times.
- Thank God for sending his Holy Spirit to be with you in the good times and the hard times.
- Confess any attitudes of prejudice, racism, or discrimination in your heart, and pray for eyes to see people as Jesus does.

- Pray for your church to follow the vision God has for
  his people in every generation.

*Great power exists in recognizing our master's voice. We must
be disciplined enough to listen and brave enough to obey.*

Between Sessions

PERSONAL REFLECTION

Take time for personal reflection, and think about the following questions …

How can you be more open and responsive to the leading of the Holy Spirit?

How can you engage more meaningfully in the life of your local church?

How can you be quicker to respond when the Holy Spirit interrupts your life and directs you in a new way? How have you been sensing the Spirit trying to nudge or guide you in a new direction?

*Being part of a church family isn't
a once-a-week commitment.*

PERSONAL PRAYER JOURNEY

Pray through Acts 2:42–47, and lift up your church and the churches in your community. Pray that each church will become more of what God wants his church to be.

_____

_____

_____

_____

_____

_____

Being part of God's church is an all-in commitment.

PERSONAL ACTIONS

Embracing God's Vision for His Church

We don't live in the first century, and God doesn't want us to invest all of our time trying to be exactly like the first-century church. At the same time, the practices and strengths of the early church are a model for us, and we can embrace these characteristics in a way that fits the world and the culture in which we live.

Reflect on each of the practices of the early church in Acts 2:42–47, and write one or two ways today's church can grow in these practices and heart attitudes.

"They devoted themselves to the apostles' teaching, to the fellowship, to the breaking of bread, and to prayer. Everyone was filled with awe, and many wonders and signs were being performed through the apostles. Now all the believers were together and held all things in common. They sold their possessions and property and distributed the proceeds to all, as any had need. Every day they devoted themselves to meeting together in the temple, and broke bread from house to house. They ate their food with joyful and sincere hearts, praising God and enjoying the favor of all the people. Every day the Lord added to their number those who were being saved" (Acts 2:42–47).

Devoted to the apostles' teaching:

* _____
* _____

Devoted to fellowship:

* _____
* _____

Devoted to breaking bread:

* _____
* _____

Devoted to prayer:

* _____
* _____

Filled with awe at the mighty work of God:

- _____
- _____

Sharing resources out of love and a deep sense of community:

- _____
- _____

Meeting regularly at public gatherings:

- _____
- _____

Breaking bread in homes:

- _____
- _____

Having joyful and sincere hearts:

- _____
- _____

Praising God:

- _____
- _____

Seeing the Lord save more and more people:

- _____
- _____

Praying for Big Transformation

The apostle Paul experienced amazing transformation when Jesus reached out to him, when he repented, and when the Holy Spirit moved in his life. Read about Paul's life in the following chapters, and identify who he was before and after his conversion.

Read Acts 7–9.

What was Paul like before he accepted Jesus and was filled with the Holy Spirit?

- _____

- _____

- _____

- _____

How did Paul change after receiving Jesus and being filled with the Spirit?

- _____

- _____

- _____

- _____

Identify a person in your life whose heart seems closed to Jesus. Commit to praying regularly for this person, and ask God to bring about a powerful transformation in his or her life. Ask for faith and confidence that he is big enough to transform the toughest people.

God can take anyone and transform his or her life.

Shattering Divisions

The more things change, the more they seem to stay the same. Prejudice, division, racism, and fractured human relationships have been around from the beginning of human history. But God calls his people to battle division and strive for unity. Read the following passages, and write down how God calls us to seek reconciliation and harmony in our relationships:

John 4:4–42

_____

_____

_____

John 17:20–26

_____

_____

_____

Galatians 3:23–29

_____

_____

_____

Ephesians 2:11–22

_____

_____

_____

If God loves all people, so can we.

DEEPER LEARNING

As you reflect on what God has been teaching you during this session, review chapters 31–35 of *The Good Book*.

JOURNAL, REFLECTIONS, AND NOTES

SESSION 8

God's Message for You

God's story in human history is still being written. The Bible is complete, but God's work in us through his Good Book is a daily adventure. If we're open to the leading of God's Spirit and responsive to biblical teachings, our character will look more and more like Jesus's. We'll find joy even in the hard times of life. We'll see God do fresh, new things in us and through us. God's message is crystal clear: he is still present, active, and alive in the world and in our lives.

THE BIG PICTURE

Session Title: God's Message for You

The Story Line: When Jesus died on the cross and rose from the grave, he offered forgiveness of sin. When he sent the Holy Spirit, he gave us the power we need for life. When God birthed his church, a new community was formed and continues to this day. The teaching of God's Good Book continues to change hearts and lives. Now we enter into that story. As we study the Bible, follow Jesus, and allow the Holy Spirit to guide us, we change and the world around us changes. God is still writing his story in and through our lives.

The Time Line: The days of the early church through today

Key Books:
- Romans
- Galatians
- James
- 1 John

Key Themes:
- True love isn't self-focused but others focused.
- When we place our faith in Jesus, we're adopted into God's family.
- God wants us to be dependent on him, not on ourselves.
- God wants to grow his character and the fruit of his Spirit in our lives.
- We can experience joy even in times of suffering if we walk close to God.
- Walking with Jesus will always lead to lasting and authentic life transformation.

Key Characters:
- Jesus
- The Holy Spirit

Prayer Direction:
- Ask God to help you grow to love his Good Book and commit to reading it daily.
- Pray for an open heart that hears God as he points out areas in your life where you need to grow and become more like Jesus.
- Invite the Holy Spirit to transform your attitudes, heart, and actions.

INTRODUCTION

Transformed

If you met Wally, you'd immediately like him. *Warm, gregarious, funny, generous,* and *faithful*—these are the words his friends would use to describe this energetic church leader. He was voted chairman of the church finance committee because of his generosity and trustworthiness. If you met Wally, you'd think he had been raised as a good church kid, known Jesus from childhood, and never wandered from the faith. But you'd be wrong!

Wally grew up on inner-city streets. He was a scrapper from his youngest days and had a reputation for winning fistfights, even with kids much larger than he. He carried his violent disposition to Vietnam, where he served in the US military. Wally actually enjoyed the violence and drugs he encountered there. He was finally removed from active duty because he was too violent. When he returned to the States, Wally became a bodyguard for a drug dealer. This gave him access to his three favorite things: drugs, violence, and women.

Will the real Wally please stand up? How can one person have lived two such radically different lives?

The answer is as profound as it is simple. Just one name: Jesus.

After years of running from God, fighting people, and indulging every hedonistic hunger in his body and soul, Wally came to the cross and met the One who loved him despite all his sins. Wally was transformed over time into a new man. He was born again, and the fruit of the Holy Spirit began to grow in his life.

TALK ABOUT IT

Tell about a person you've met who went through a dramatic and shocking transformation after coming to faith in Jesus.

Or

Tell about one way God has transformed you (or is transforming you) into a new person as you grow in faith.

We don't become holy through our own efforts.

VIDEO TEACHING NOTES

The purpose of the Bible

Cole's story

Spiritual adoption (becoming God's children and brothers and sisters in God's family)

Christy's story

A powerful metaphor for the human heart: a
garage

Evidence of the Holy Spirit's work in our lives:

- The fruit of the Spirit leading to character changes
- Joy in suffering
- Life transformation

VIDEO DISCUSSION

1. Respond to this statement: "The primary purpose of the Bible
is to help us become more like Jesus." How does this statement
match up with how many people see the Bible? How does it affect
your desire to read the Bible?

> *The Bible is more than ink on paper; it's*
> *God's living and active Word.*

2. How did you see the heart of Jesus in the way people treated
Cole and included him on the football team (and in their lives)?
Tell about a time in your life when you saw someone serve, include,
and love others like Jesus does.

> *Our destiny is to become like Jesus in our actions and attitudes.*

Read Romans 8:14–17 and Ephesians 1:3–6.

3. What are some of the powerful and positive images that
accompany the idea of being adopted into God's spiritual family?

How have you experienced these realities since you were adopted into God's family? If God has truly adopted us and made us his children, how should this affect our relationships with other Christians in our church and even those in other Christian congregations?

4. If you've ever felt abandoned by a person, an organization, or even a local church, how did that experience affect your life? How can feeling abandoned by people make us feel as though we've been abandoned by God as well? Why is it dangerous to believe that being rejected by people is the same as being rejected by God?

5. In the ancient Roman world, when a person was adopted, two very important things happened: (1) the person became an heir of the family estate, with all the corresponding rights; and (2) all of the person's debts were wiped out, and he or she was given a fresh start. What are the spiritual implications of these two realities for those who receive Jesus and are adopted into the family of God? What do we inherit when we become children of God through faith in Jesus? What is wiped away?

When we become children of God, the promotion brings with it a promise: God will watch over us, leading us faithfully through the events and circumstances of this life.

6. In Christy's story, she talked about the point in her life when she finally realized she had to be dependent on God and not on herself,

alcohol, or other people. Tell about a point in your life when it became clear that you needed to be fully dependent on God. What gets in the way of living each day with a firm conviction that you need to depend on God at all times for all things?

In times of suffering and struggle, we discover
that we're never alone. God is with us.

7. Jesus has power to set us free from any bondage we're experiencing. In what area of life are you feeling spiritual bondage? How can group members pray for you and support you as you seek to live in the freedom of Jesus in this area?

No one is too far gone to experience God's grace.

8. Christy talked about a moment when she had been walking with Jesus and growing in faith and it dawned on her, *This is a great life!* Tell about a time it struck you that following Jesus and living close to him is actually an amazing way to live. What can you do to walk closer with Jesus and create more moments when you experience the goodness of being a child of God?

9. Deron painted a powerful picture of the way garages get filled with junk and how this can happen to our hearts as well. We can have so much useless junk packed in our garages that there's no room for what matters most. What are some of the things we can collect in our hearts that can push out the One who matters most?

List one or two things you need to toss out of your heart to make more room for Jesus.

Left to our own devices, we'll never see change in our lives.

Read Galatians 5:22–26.

10. What is one fruit of the Spirit that is growing and blossoming in your life right now? How are you seeing God grow this fruit, and why does this bring you joy? What is a fruit of the Spirit that really needs to grow in your life? What steps can you take to cultivate this fruit in your life?

Read James 1:2–4.

11. Tell about a time you went through loss, pain, or suffering and God showed up, bringing real and deep joy into your life during this season. How can hard times in life be a perfect environment to grow your faith and deepen your joy?

Challenges bring with them the opportunity to develop maturity.

Read 1 John 3:1–2.

12. How are you experiencing life transformation right now? Where is God at work? In what area of your life do you believe God wants to do a new work in you? How can group members pray for you, cheer you on, and hold you accountable?

God's Spirit is the source and sustenance of any lasting change in our character as we follow the person of Jesus.

CLOSING PRAYER

Take time as a group to pray in some of the following directions ...

- Thank God for what he has taught you during these eight sessions of *The Good Book*.
- Pray for your church to be a body of believers who embrace people and love them in the name of Jesus.
- Thank God for adopting you as his child through Jesus, and pray for power to live a life that honors your Father.
- Thank God for the amazing inheritance he has given you.
- Ask the Holy Spirit to grow all the fruit he wants to see fully developed in your life.

Instead of praying, "God, get me out of this!" choose to pray, "God, what do you want me to get out of this?"

Between Sessions

PERSONAL REFLECTION

Take time for personal reflection, and think about the following questions …

Think of one person you know who is often left out and marginalized. What can you do to include this person and encourage God's family to embrace him or her?

What debts has God wiped out because you've placed your faith in Jesus? How can you express your joy and appreciation for this amazing gift?

Describe some of the junk piled up in the garage of your heart. How can you clean out that junk to make more room for Jesus?

Too often we fill our hearts with junk.

PERSONAL PRAYER JOURNEY

God desires to bring about transformation in our attitudes and actions. Identify a couple of attitudes and actions in your life that need to be transformed. Pray for insight from the Word of God to guide you to the right path and for the power of the Spirit to move you to action.

_____

_____

_____

_____

God can use any circumstance or crisis to make us more like Christ.

PERSONAL ACTIONS

One Another, One Another!
Many passages in the Bible call us to live in community with one another in various ways. Read each of the following passages, and note the "one another" messages you find.

John 13:34–35

_____

_____

Romans 12:10

_____

_____

Romans 12:16

_____

_____

Romans 15:7

_____

_____

Romans 15:14

_____

_____

Galatians 5:13

_____

_____

Ephesians 4:32

_____

_____

Colossians 3:13

_____

_____

Colossians 3:16

_____

_____

1 Thessalonians 5:11

_____

_____

Hebrews 10:25

_____

_____

Identify one or two areas in which you need to grow in your relationship with other believers. Pray for power to grow in these areas.

Fruit Check

"But the fruit of the Spirit is love, joy, peace, patience, kindness, goodness, faithfulness, gentleness, and self-control" (Gal. 5:22–23).

God wants all the fruit of the Holy Spirit to grow in our lives. We experience this as our faith in Jesus deepens. Ask God to grow his fruit in your life, and write down what you can do to develop these aspects of your Christian character.

Love

_____

_____

Joy

_____

_____

Peace

_____

_____

Patience

_____

_____

Kindness

_____

_____

Goodness

_____

_____

Faithfulness

_____

_____

Gentleness

_____

_____

Self-control

_____

_____

Life Transformation … the Hard Places

We all have one or two areas of our lives where God is knocking on the door, nudging us, or even pushing us hard to repent and begin living in a new way. It can be a bad attitude, an action we need to take, or a sin that needs to be dealt with and driven out.

> **Pray for revelation—*Search me, Lord.*** Take time to pray and ask God's Spirit to reveal an area in your life that needs to change. Commit to responding to God's leading as he shows you where he wants to bring transformation.

> **Cry out for help—*Give me power.*** Once you have a clear sense of where God wants you to change, admit your inability to overcome this struggle, and cry out to God for power to live in a new way that will honor and glorify him.

> **Ask others to hold you accountable—*Help me.*** Invite one or two trusted Christian friends to pray for you, hold you accountable, and challenge you as you seek to grow in this area of your life.

> **Celebrate growth—*Praise you, God.*** When you experience some noticeable transformation in your life, share some testimonies, lift up prayers of praise, sing a song, have some good food,

rejoice in God's power to change his children. Get together with friends who are supporting you and have a little celebration!

Resembling Jesus is a daily challenge; it's also our destiny.

DEEPER LEARNING

As you reflect on what God has been teaching you during this session, review chapters 36–40 of *The Good Book*.

JOURNAL, REFLECTIONS, AND NOTES

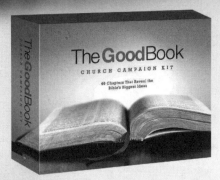